SHANIA TWAIN

by
Jill C. Wheeler

Visit us at
www.abdopub.com

Published by ABDO Publishing Company, 4940 Viking
Drive, Edina, MN 55435. Copyright ©2001 by Abdo
Consulting Group, Inc. International copyrights reserved in
all countries. No part of this book may be reproduced in
any form without written permission from the publisher.

Printed in the United States.

Graphic Design: John Hamilton
Cover Design: MacLean Tuminelly
Cover photo: Shooting Stars
Interior photos:
   AP/Wide World, p. 39, 51, 53
   Corbis, p. 5, 6, 10-11, 13, 16, 17, 18, 21, 27, 28, 31, 33,
      43, 45, 47, 55, 56, 59, 60-61, 63
   Mercury, p. 32
   Mercury Nashville, p. 38, 42, 50, 54, 57
   Shooting Stars, p. 4, 25, 34-35, 37, 41
   Time Pix, p. 9, 15, 49, 52

Library of Congress Cataloging-in-Publication Data
Wheeler, Jill C., 1964-
      Shania Twain / Jill C. Wheeler.
         p. cm. — (Star tracks)
      Includes index.
      ISBN 1-57765-552-4
      1. Twain, Shania—Juvenile literature. 2. Singers—
Canada—Biography—Juvenile literature. [1. Twain, Shania.
2. Singers. 3. Women—Biography.] I. Title. II. Series

ML3930.T88 W44 2001
782.421642'092—dc21
[B]
                                                00-069988

CONTENTS

New Star in Nashville 4

Prospector's Daughter 8

Little Girl, Big Guitar 14

The Long, Hard Road 20

Tragedy Strikes 26

"Shania Twain" 32

A New Partner 36

Breaking Records 44

Answering Critics 48

Still the One 54

Where on the Web? 62

Glossary 63

Index 64

NEW
STAR
IN NASHVILLE

COUNTRY MUSIC FANS' EYES WERE ON Los Angeles on May 3, 2000. It was the annual Academy of Country Music Awards gala. Country Music Hall of Fame member Dolly Parton hosted the three-hour event. Thousands of fans tuned in to find out who would win the year's awards.

The time came to give the Entertainer of the Year award. Parton accepted the honor on behalf of the winner, Shania (shu-Nye-uh) Twain, who was at her home in Switzerland. "Shania couldn't be here tonight, she's out of the country," said the country music legend. "We accept this award on her behalf. Maybe I can take it to her and meet her."

Parton's remarks were funny for anyone who knew much about Shania Twain. The 34-year-old singer had been a fan of Dolly Parton for most of her life. In fact, Dolly had been famous in country music almost since Shania was born. In September 1999, while accepting the Entertainer of the Year award from the prestigious Country Music Association, Shania said she wanted to meet her lifelong idol, Parton!

"Shania is now one of the most recognized names in country music."

It's very likely the two will meet someday. Shania Twain is now one of the most recognized names in country music. Two of her three albums have sold more than 10 million copies—the most ever for a female country singer. Her song "You're Still the One" became an international hit. Her world tour sold out. Many people consider her among the most innovative artists in country music today.

"Shania's a worldwide artist," says country singer Faith Hill. "It's clear that she's broken down a lot of walls, and shattered every record, even competing with the men, which is such an incredible accomplishment."

The road to stardom hasn't been easy for this Canadian native. Though only in her thirties, Shania's success took more than 20 years of hard work and sacrifice. Throughout that time, she never let anything stop her.

PROSPECTOR'S DAUGHTER

SHANIA TWAIN WAS BORN EILLEEN Regina Edwards on August 28, 1965, in Windsor, Ontario, Canada. She was the second of three girls born to Clarence Edwards, a railroad engineer, and his wife, Sharon. Shania's parents divorced when she was just a toddler. Sharon took her girls and moved to Timmins, Ontario. Timmins is a goldmining town in the woods about 500 miles north of Toronto. Shania never heard much from her father again.

A few years later, Sharon met and married Jerry Twain. Jerry was a full-blooded Native American of the Ojibwa tribe. He worked in Timmins as a forester and a prospector. He adopted Shania, her older sister, Jill, and younger sister, Carrie-Ann. Later he and Sharon had two boys of their own, Mark and Darryl.

> **"The thing that made Shania different from everyone else in her family was the way she loved to sing."**

Life in Timmins was hard at times. Jerry couldn't always find regular work. Many times the family had little money. Shania says she can remember packing mustard sandwiches in her lunchbox because the family couldn't afford meat. She didn't want her teachers to see how little she had to eat some days. She was afraid they'd try to take her away from her family if they did.

There were many happy times for Shania as well. Since her stepfather adopted her and her sisters, Shania was considered a member of the Ojibwa tribe. She grew up learning about their culture and way of life.

That included a love of nature and the outdoors. As a child, Shania learned how to set snares for rabbits and helped her father hunt in the woods. Shania grew to love time alone in the wilderness.

But the thing that made Shania different from everyone else in her family was the way she loved to sing. Even at age three she would sing along with the local jukebox. Not only would she sing the melody, but she also would harmonize. Sometimes it seemed like she never stopped singing. "Shania would always be singing, even just walking down the street," recalled Carrie-Ann. "I'd be embarrassed."

Sharon Twain was not embarrassed. In fact, she was thrilled. It became clear her middle daughter had a special talent. It became Sharon's quest to see that talent grow to its fullest potential. "My mother lived for my career," Shania said. "We were extremely poor when I was a kid, and my mother was often depressed with five children and no food to feed them. She knew I was talented and she lived with the hope that my abilities were my chance to do something special."

"Shania would always be singing, even just walking down the street."

LITTLE GIRL, BIG GUITAR

BOTH SHARON AND JERRY TWAIN enjoyed country-western music. It often was playing in their home. "My parents were obsessed with country music," Shania said. "I grew up listening to Waylon (Jennings), Willie (Nelson), Dolly (Parton), Tammy (Wynette), all of them."

When Shania was in first grade, she performed "Take Me Home Country Roads" for her class. The song had been a hit for John Denver. It was one of Shania's favorite songs. Unfortunately, her classmates didn't like it. They made fun of her for singing what they considered a country song. They even teased her with a new nickname—"Twang."

"Shania began writing her own songs when she was 10."

At home, Shania's family encouraged her musical abilities. Jerry had taught himself to play the guitar. He taught Shania the basics when she could barely get her small arms around the instrument. While she was learning guitar from her father, her mother was setting up times and places for her to perform.

"From the age of eight, I was doing weekends, the odd gig here and there," Shania said. "I did everything my parents could get me on. Every TV station, every radio station, every community center, every old age home. They had me doing everything."

Sometimes her parents would wake her up in the middle of the night so she could perform in a nightclub. "I used to be dragged out of bed in the morning and they'd bring me to the local club to play with the band," she said. "They couldn't allow me in a liquor premise before 1:00 a.m., when they stopped serving. I'd get up and sing a few songs with the band and before I knew it I was actually doing clubs professionally."

Sharon would dress Shania in denim skirts and buckskin-fringed vests for her club gigs. People began to talk about the little girl with the big guitar.

England's Prince Charles talks with Shania after her stage performance in London in 1999.

"Even when Shania was performing three nights a week, she still got her work in on time."

In her teens, her mother drove her the 500 miles to Toronto for voice lessons whenever the family could afford it. Shania felt guilty about the extra time and money her family was spending on her. She vowed to make it worth their while. She felt she had the power to help bring in more money, even as a child.

Shania's drive to excel caused her to act older than her years. When she was 10 years old, her school principal asked her to sing at an event after school. Shania agreed, then she went on to list all of the sound equipment she would need. She also suggested that the principal arrange for Shania's performance with her mother.

Shania began writing her own songs when she was 10. "I liked to escape my personal life through my music," she said. "Music was all I ever did. I spent a lot of time in solitude with just my guitar, writing and singing away for hours. I would play 'til my fingers were bruised, and I loved it!"

Her focus on music left time for little else. While she loved playing sports, she didn't have much time for them. She also had to squeeze her homework in somewhere. Even when she was performing three nights a week, she still got her work in on time.

THE LONG, HARD ROAD

IN 1978, SHARON ARRANGED FOR SHANIA to open for a Canadian country singer named Mary Bailey. Bailey was a friend of Sharon's. Bailey remembers the first time she saw Shania on stage. Barely 12, she was singing a Hank Williams classic, "I'm So Lonesome I Could Cry."

"She was this little girl who got on stage with a guitar and just blew me away," Bailey said. Bailey, who had released two singles on RCA Records, never forgot the emotion she saw in the young singer.

Shania's performance earned the same reaction from another young musician. After hearing 16-year-old Shania, he invited her to audition to sing with his rock band, Longshot. "We wouldn't let her leave the audition until she promised to join the band," he said. "There was such power in her voice. It was such an adult voice for someone so young."

Longshot had a successful run at local high
school and community events. It kept Shania
performing, though it didn't pay many bills. She
still took jobs at McDonald's and Sears to help her
family. She also spent summers helping her father
with his new reforestation business. There the
5-foot, 4-inch woman learned to use a chainsaw
and an axe, working as a foreman for a roughneck
13-member crew. Most teens would have
complained about the work or refused to do it. Not
Shania.

Whenever she could, Shania stole away with
her friends to concerts. Seeing Van Halen in
concert was an experience she never forgot.
Shania also missed her own high school
graduation in 1983 because Longshot was on
the road.

"There was such power in her voice. It was such an adult voice for someone so young."

After high school, Sharon asked Mary Bailey to help Shania get a record contract. Shania had been to Nashville once before with no success. Mary took her again. Once again, they were turned down. The people in country music weren't interested in a teenage singer. Besides, Shania was having too much fun performing rock and pop hits. She continued to play gigs around Timmins and even down to Toronto.

Eventually, Shania had to make a decision. She knew the only way she could truly succeed in show business was to leave Timmins and move to Toronto. In the city, she got a job as a secretary during the day and spent her weekends working on her music. She played with many different bands and even opened for a touring Broadway show. In the spring and summer, she traded in her sequined gowns to go back to Timmins and help Jerry with his reforestation business.

TRAGEDY

STRIKES

IN NOVEMBER 1987, SHANIA WAS BACK in Toronto working on her music. Then she received a phone call that changed everything. It was her older sister, Jill. She told Shania that Sharon and Jerry had been killed. They had been coming back from a reforestation site when their truck crashed head-on into a logging truck. Both died instantly.

Shania knew at once that she had to return home. Jill had her own family. Shania was the logical one to take care of Carrie-Ann, Mark, and Darryl, all of whom were still at home. The responsibility frightened her, but she took on the role of mom. She even screened Carrie-Ann's boyfriends. Mark says Shania was very strict with them because she was so scared. "I was on automatic pilot, doing what I had to do," Shania said. "It was a stressful time."

"Despite her responsibilities, Shania refused to give up her dream."

Despite her responsibilities, Shania refused to give up her dream—or her music. She sold her parent's house in Timmins and moved the family to Huntsville, Ontario. There, with Mary Bailey's help, she landed a job at a place called Deerhurst Resort. Deerhurst put on Las Vegas-style shows. Shania could continue performing without having to travel. Plus, she would earn a regular paycheck.

Deerhurst was a great opportunity for Shania. She had the chance to perform many different kinds of music. She learned about staging and choreography. Her on-stage persona became more polished. Because the people at the resort were on vacation, Shania never had "regular" fans. She learned to win people over anew each night.

Life outside of Deerhurst was still a challenge for the Twains. The plumbing in their house didn't always work. Sometimes they had to bathe in the river, or Shania would haul water from Deerhurst. Shania juggled working at Deerhurst with taking her brothers to and from school and their other engagements with the family's lone pick-up truck.

Shania worked at Deerhurst for three years until her siblings had moved out on their own. When they were gone, she suddenly felt like an old woman whose children had left the nest. "I had all this time on my hands," she said. "I didn't have to cook and clean for anybody... It was like, 'I'm free!' I said, 'Now what am I gonna do with my life?' I decided I wanted to go for it."

For the next step in her career, Shania called upon her old friend Mary Bailey. Mary arranged for Nashville agent Dick Frank to come see Shania at Deerhurst. He liked what he saw, and took her to Nashville to introduce her to producer Norro Wilson. Wilson helped Shania record several songs that got the attention of Harold Shedd at Mercury Records. Shedd signed her to a recording contract in 1991.

Shedd also suggested that the singer, still known as Eilleen Twain, change her name. Shania recalled a woman who worked with her at Deerhurst. Her name was the Ojibwa word for "I'm on my way." Eilleen became Shania, and moved to Nashville. Now she truly was on her way.

"I said, 'Now what am I gonna do with my life?' I decided I wanted to go for it."

"SHANIA TWAIN"

SHANIA'S FIRST ALBUM, "SHANIA TWAIN," was released in 1993. Shania wrote only one of the songs on the album. Critics agree the song she wrote, "God Ain't Gonna Getcha For That" is the best on the album. The rest of the songs were standard country fare.

"Shania Twain" showcased Shania's impressive voice. However, it stopped there. The record company did its best to promote the album and Shania. Among the efforts was a music video for the song "What Made You Say That." The video featured Shania on a Florida beach frolicking with a shirtless man.

Shania Twain

"Shania Twain" sold about 100,000 copies. It gave Shania national and international exposure. Country Music Television in Europe gave Shania its Rising Star Award.

As it turned out, the best thing that came from "Shania Twain" was the video for "What Made You Say That." It was playing one day on Country Music Television Europe when veteran music producer Robert John "Mutt" Lange noticed it. He picked up the phone in his home in England and made a call that changed Shania's life. It was spring of 1993.

A NEW PARTNER

ROBERT JOHN LANGE, OR MUTT, AS HE had been called since childhood, had produced a string of highly successful rock albums. His songwriting and musical genius was behind the success of such groups as AC/DC, Def Leppard and Bryan Adams. Originally from South Africa, he now was at home in England. He and Shania began to talk almost daily over the phone. She would sing her songs to him, and he would sing back and offer suggestions.

After months of phone calls, Mutt traveled to the United States to meet Shania in June 1993. Shania only intended to work with Mutt professionally. Yet only a few weeks after meeting him face-to-face, she changed her mind. "We knew we wanted to be together for the rest of our lives," she said.

The two were married on December 28, 1993, in Huntsville, Ontario. By that time, they already had written half an album's worth of songs. They continued working on the album as they traveled together through the United States, Canada, England, Spain, Italy, and the Caribbean. Mutt intended to record a top-notch album for Shania featuring her original songs. For Shania, it was a dream come true to have a skilled and respected producer like Mutt believe so strongly in her work.

That dream album was "The Woman In Me." Shania wrote almost all of the songs. She wrote "You Win My Love" especially for her husband.

The first single, "Whose Bed Have Your Boots Been Under" entered the Billboard Country Singles chart in January 1995. The album was  released the following month. The single rocketed to No. 11 on the chart and the album quickly was certified gold. Four more Shania Twain songs became number one hits within 20 weeks, each at the top of the singles chart.

The Woman
In Me

Shania elected not to tour to promote the album, but she did do videos. She and Mutt worked with noted photographer John Derek to create a special image for Shania. She wanted to be seen as an elegant yet earthy outdoorswoman. She didn't hesitate to showcase her beauty and athletic physique. Her belly-button-baring outfits had some in the country music industry shaking their heads.

Shania also was criticized for her relationship with Mutt. Some claimed she was a puppet, only doing what he asked her. "The Woman In Me" had been the most expensive country album ever produced. Mutt paid for a lot of the costs. Shania didn't take time to listen to the naysayers. She had poured her heart and soul into the album. She felt it represented her true self, and that she and Mutt were equal partners.

"Shania poured her heart and soul into 'The Woman In Me.'"

The final song on the album was perhaps the song closest to Shania. It is called "God Bless The Child." "That song is a lullaby I wrote after my parents died," Shania said. "I would go for long walks in the bush by myself with this song swimming around in my head. I really don't know where the melody came from. When I met Mutt, I sang it for him and he said, 'Wow, that's beautiful!' We didn't even change it. There's no chorus, no verse.... It's just a true sincere thought and emotion."

Shania donated the proceeds from "God Bless The Child" to Kids Cafe/Second Harvest Food Bank in the U.S. and the Canadian Living

Foundation. The Foundation provides meals for underprivileged children just like she had once been.

God Bless The Child

BREAKING

RECORDS

THERE WAS NO STOPPING SHANIA AFTER "The Woman In Me." As Christmas 1995 approached, the album had been certified four times platinum. It would go on to sell more than 12 million copies. That puts Shania in the ranks of other female superstars such as Alanis Morissette, Whitney Houston, and Carole King. "The Woman In Me" also spent 29 weeks at the top of Billboard's Top Country Albums Chart. That was a new record that surpassed even Wynonna Judd and Mary Chapin Carpenter.

Shania now was one of the hottest young female star in country music with a happy marriage and a future full of promise. She and Mutt purchased a home in upstate New York where Shania could spend time alone in the woods as she loved to do. They added a stable for Shania's other passion: horses. A recording studio on the grounds of their estate meant they could continue to partner on new efforts.

When not at home, Shania was making many public appearances and performances. She attracted more than 10,000 fans for an appearance at the Mall of America in Minneapolis, Minnesota. She appeared on The Oprah Winfrey Show.

Her presence also was in demand at many award shows. She was on stage at the American Music Awards in January 1996, where she was named Favorite New Country Artist. She had to decline performing at the Juno Awards, the Canadian equivalent of the Grammy Awards, due to the flu. However, she still won awards for Country Female Vocalist of the Year and Entertainer of the Year.

At America's own Grammy Awards, Shania won Best Country Album in 1996 for "The Woman In Me." The Billboard Music Award for Country Album of the Year also went to Shania in 1996.

Shania won the 1996 Best Country Album Grammy Award for "The Woman In Me."

ANSWERING
CRITICS

IT SEEMS THERE ARE ALWAYS A FEW people who resent it when a person is successful. So it seemed with Shania. Shortly after her success at the Juno Awards, her former hometown newspaper printed a story about her natural father. The newspaper claimed Shania had turned her back on Clarence Edwards. It also claimed she pretended to be part Native American when she really was not.

Shania fought back. She admitted she hadn't always told people she was Jerry's adopted daughter. She also said her background shouldn't be everyone else's business. "Half the people in my life didn't know I was adopted," she said. "Why should I have told the press?"

To cope, Shania returned to what she loved most. She spent what time she could in the woods. And she hit the stage. Her five-song set at Nashville's annual Fan Fair was the hit of the event. She also traveled to New York City for appearances with Rosie O'Donnell and Late Night with Conan O'Brien.

Back in Canada, her hometown didn't let the media controversy get in the way of their appreciation. The leaders of Timmins made August 15, 1996, Shania Twain Day. They even renamed a street Shania Twain Way.

That fall, it was time for the Country Music Association Awards. The CMAs are the most coveted awards in the business. Shania had been nominated for three CMAs in 1995 but had not won any. This year, she was nominated another three times for Female Vocalist of the Year, Song

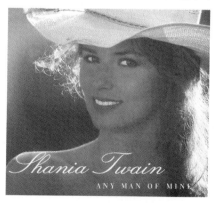

of the Year for "Any Man Of Mine," and the Horizon Award, which honors creative growth.

Any Man Of Mine

Shania performing at the 1998 Country Music Association Awards.

Shania went to the awards alone. Mutt hates publicity and public appearances. "He's a very humble guy and basically doesn't want to be a star," Shania said. "He just wants to be a person who makes music." Sadly, Shania left alone—and empty-handed. It was a slap in her face that an album as successful as "The Woman In Me" still had not found favor in the eyes of the country music establishment.

Shania took the awards program in stride. Instead of moping, she and Mutt got busy on another album.

STILL THE

O N E

"COME ON OVER" WAS THE NEXT ALBUM for Shania. She and Mutt wrote all 16 songs. "Writing's like coloring to me," she said. "Kids like to color. They don't need to have a reason to color; they just like it. That's how I feel about songwriting. It's a chance to just create without inhibitions."

Shania wasn't sure how fans would react, but she knew the album was one she could be proud of. "I like to use phrases people use everyday," she explained. "I wanted this album to be conversational. The lyrics are not going to get you an 'A' in grammar, that's for sure. But it's more the way we speak in everyday life."

SHANIA TWAIN
COME ON OVER

Come On Over

Shania shows off her prize at the 1998 Country Music Association Awards.

*Shania with her 1998
Billboard Music Awards.*

"Come On Over" includes the smash international hit "You're Still The One." Shania wrote the song for Mutt. Because she and Mutt lead such busy lives, they don't always see much of each other. That's led to rumors that their marriage is rocky. Shania quickly denies it.

She admits she and Mutt are opposites in many ways. They are from different backgrounds. He spent most of his career working in rock music. She's always been a country music girl. He is 16 years older than she is. She loves publicity. He avoids it. Yet their marriage works. "He's given me the confidence to be who I am," she said. "He really is Mr. Wonderful."

Shania's fans found "Come On Over" to be pretty wonderful as well. It hit record stores in November 1997. The first single, "Love Gets Me Every Time" went gold in the U.S. in just five weeks.

SHANIA TWAIN
you're still the one

You're Still The One

This time, Shania decided to tour in support of the album. She wanted to show critics she could put on a live show as well as record in the studio. She kicked off the tour in May 1998 near her hometown in Ontario. Her two-plus-hour concerts quickly proved she had the charisma and staying power to succeed on the road. The tour sold more than a million tickets worldwide. She also made sure that a portion of the proceeds was donated to local charities that help hungry kids. Her band toured for over a year. In addition, the album has sold more than 18 million copies. That makes it the best-selling album in the history of country music, and the top-selling album by a female solo artist.

In 1999, Shania and Mutt moved to a chateau in Switzerland. That September, Shania finally won her long-deserved recognition at the CMA awards. She took home the award for Entertainer of the Year. She was the first woman in 13 years to receive such an honor. Shania's fans have no doubt she'll do it again.

A teary-eyed Shania Twain thanks her supporters at the Country Music Awards in Nashville after receiving the 1999 Entertainer of the Year award.

WHERE ON THE WEB?

You can find out more about Shania Twain by visiting the following web sites:

Shania Twain Online Fan Club
http:www.shania.org

Shania Twain Shrine
http://www.musicfanclubs.org/shania/

Wall of Sound: Shania Twain
http://wallofsound.go.com/artists/
shaniatwain.home.html

Shania Twain Official PolyGram Records Site
http://www.shania-twain.com/

GLOSSARY

Bush: Land that's a long way away from cities and towns.

Gig: A job or booking for musicians.

Gold record: A record that sells more than 500,000 copies.

Platinum record: A record that sells more than one million copies.

Shania Twain presents the Entertainer of the Year award at the 2000 Country Music Association Awards in Nashville.

INDEX

A
AC/DC 36
Academy of Country Music 4
Adams, Bryan 36
American Music Awards 46
"Any Man Of Mine" 50

B
Bailey, Mary 20, 24, 29, 30
Billboard 38, 44, 46
Billboard Music Awards 46

C
Canada 8, 38, 50
Canadian Living Foundation 42
Caribbean 38
Carpenter, Mary Chapin 44
"Come On Over" 54, 57
Country Music Association
   6, 50, 58
Country Music Association
   Awards 50, 58
Country Music Hall of Fame 4
Country Music Television 35

D
Deerhurst Resort 29, 30
Def Leppard 36
Denver, John 14
Derek, John 40

E
Edwards, Clarence 8, 48
Edwards, Eileen 8, 30
England 35, 36, 38

F
Fan Fair 50
Florida 32
Frank, Dick 30

G
"God Bless The Child" 42
"God Ain't Gonna Getcha For
   That" 32
Grammy Awards 46

H
Hill, Faith 7
Horizon Award 50

Houston, Whitney 44
Huntsville, Ontario, Canada 29,
   38

I
Italy 38

J
Jennings, Waylon 14
Judd, Wynonna 44
Juno Awards 46, 48

K
Kids Cafe/Second Harvest
   Food Bank 42
King, Carole 44

L
Lange, Robert John "Mutt" 35,
   36, 38, 40, 42, 44, 53, 54, 57,
   58
Las Vegas, Nevada 29
Late Night with Conan 50
Longshot 20, 23
Los Angeles 4
"Love Gets Me Every Time" 57

M
Mall of America 46
McDonald's 23
Minneapolis, Minnesota 46
Morissette, Alanis 44

N
Nashville, Tennessee 24, 30, 50
Nelson, Willie 14
New York 44
New York City 50

O
Ojibwa 8, 11, 30
Ontario, Canada 8, 29, 38, 58

P
Parton, Dolly 4, 6, 14

R
RCA Records 20
Rising Star Award 35
Rosie, O'Donnell 50

S
Sears 23
"Shania Twain" 32, 35
Shania Twain Day 50
Shania Twain Way 50
Shedd, Harold 30
"I'm So Lonesome I Could
   20
South Africa 36
Spain 38
"You're Still The One" 7
Switzerland 4, 58

T
"Take Me Home Country
   14
The Oprah Winfrey Show
"The Woman In Me" 38,
   46, 53
Timmins, Ontario, Canada
   24, 29, 50
Toronto, Canada 8, 19,
Twain, Carrie-Ann 8, 12
Twain, Darryl 8, 26
Twain, Jerry 8, 11, 14, 16,
   26, 48
Twain, Jill 8, 26
Twain, Mark 8, 26
Twain, Sharon 8, 12, 14, 1
   24, 26

U
United States 36, 38, 42,

V
Van Halen 23

W
"What Made You Say That
   35
"Whose Bed Have Your Bc
   Been Under" 38
Williams, Hank 20
Wilson, Norro 30
Windsor, Ontario, Canada
Wynette, Tammy 14

Y
"You Win My Love" 38